COUTURE OR TRADE

AN EARLY PICTORIAL RECORD OF THE

LONDON COLLEGE OF FASHION

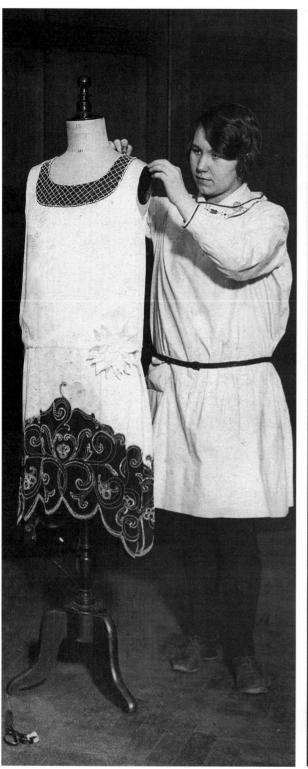

Students using the stand in the 1920s and 1950s respectively.

COUTURE OR TRADE

AN EARLY PICTORIAL RECORD OF THE
LONDON COLLEGE OF FASHION

Helen Reynolds

Phillimore

1997

Published by
PHILLIMORE & CO. LTD.,
Shopwyke Manor Barn, Chichester, West Sussex

ISBN 1 86077 066 5

Printed and bound in Great Britain by
BIDDLES LTD.
Guildford, Surrey

LIST OF ILLUSTRATIONS

Frontispiece: Using the stand

ACKNOWLEDGEMENTS

I would like to thank first and foremost Jane Holt, Special Collections Librarian at the London College of Fashion, who was the major instigator of this project. Her help, support and expertise were invaluable and made this project possible.

I would also like to thank Katherine Baird, Head of Learning Resources, London College of Fashion, for her encouragement and for furnishing me with the excellent title *Trade or Couture*; James Rutherford for photographing the students' textile samples, and all the library staff for their friendly advice and help.

I have also benefited from the expertise of many friends, in particular, Jean Mitchell and Joslyn [Molly] Baker. The advice of Elizabeth Rouse and discussions within the Cultural and Historical Studies Research Group at London College of Fashion have been of great help.

This book would not have been possible without all the former staff and students who allowed me to interview them. Oral histories have played a major part in this project and I owe a particular debt of gratitude to all those whom I interviewed. They include Miss Lily Silverberg, Miss Mary Wildman, Mrs. May Thornton [assisted by Mr. Henry Thornton, a tailoring student at Regents Park Polytechnic], Miss Renee Baxter, Miss Yvonne Dyer, Mrs. J. Alexander, Mrs. Jenny Rosner and others too numerous to mention.

For permission to reproduce photographs I would like to thank the London College of Fashion Learning Resources Department. I am also grateful to the London Metropolitan Archives [formerly the Greater London Records Office] for their generous permission to reproduce pictures from their collection.

The following have also generously allowed the reproduction of photographs from newspaper archives: Popperfoto for plate 167; Times Newspapers Ltd. for the *Daily Sketch* pictures, 32, 34, 35, 45, 46 and 61; Trevor York at Solo Syndication for the *Daily Mail* pictures, 57, 58, 65, 69-72 and Express Newspapers for plate 75. In all cases copyright remains with them.

Although every attempt has been made to trace the copyright holders of the photographs, the London College of Fashion Learning Resources Department and the author apologise in advance for any unintentional omission or neglect.

Finally I would like to thank my family, Paul, Claire, Christopher, Laurie and Rhicert for supporting me through this project.

FOREWORD

The photographs in this book are confined to the training given to women in needle-trades courses at three trade schools in London. These schools were of a number of British trade schools that provided artisan training for both boys and girls in the first half of the 20th century. The schools were usually situated in an area where there was an established industry which the pupils could enter. Boys' trade schools offered courses which included cabinet making, silver smithing, printing and bespoke men's tailoring. Girls predominantly received a training in occupations that had traditionally employed women. Barrett Street Trade School, for example, ran a highly successful ladies' hairdressing course whilst Clapham Trade School offered a course in tea room cookery. Other girls' trade schools offered courses in photography, corset and lingerie making, various branches of cookery and domestic service.

Our intention in publishing these photographs is that they can be enjoyed by a wider audience, but we also hope to get feed-back about the students featured in these pictures and their subsequent careers. If you have any further information, please contact the author by letter via The London College of Fashion Library, 20 John Princes Street, London, W1M 0BJ.

INTRODUCTION

The London College of Fashion has its origins in three London trade schools: Barrett Street Trade School, Shoreditch Institute Girls Trade School and Clapham Trade School. There is, in the college archive, a remarkable collection of photographs which records some of the work produced in these schools. Needle-trade schools have now been largely forgotten except by their former students. They did, however, provide one of the first examples of formal training for entry into the fashion trade. Founded at the turn of the century, most needle-trade schools were in London, but there were some successful ones in the provinces. They trained girls, from the age of twelve, for skilled jobs in the needle-trades. The schools remained open until after the Second World War when, under the 1944 Education Act, specialised training was no longer offered until general secondary education had been completed. The schools were either closed, amalgamated with other institutions or turned into technical colleges. In their time, needle-trade schools provided the West End of London's clothing trade with much of its skilled work force.

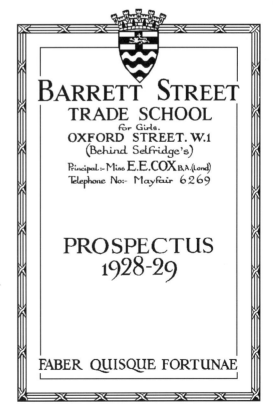

L.C.C. Barrett Street, Trade School
OXFORD STREET, W.1.

ANNUAL EXHIBITION

The Head Mistress, Staff and Students request the honour of your presence on WEDNESDAY, DECEMBER 15th, between 2 and 4.30 p.m. or 6 and 8.30 p.m.

The Students will be engaged at their respective trades and their finished work will be on view :—

> DRESSMAKING
> EMBROIDERY (Hand and Machine)
> LADIES' TAILORING
> HAIRDRESSING (Board and Saloon Work)
> FASHION SKETCHING AND DESIGN

Those interested in the work of the Junior Students or the Part-time Learners should visit the Curzon Annexe before proceeding to Barret Street.

BARRETT STREET
TRADE SCHOOL
for Girls.
OXFORD STREET. W.1
(Behind Selfridge's)
Principal :- Miss E.E.COX B.A.(Lond)
Telephone No:- Mayfair 6269

PROSPECTUS
1928-29

FABER QUISQUE FORTUNAE

1 *Above.* Invitation card for Barrett Street Trade School Annual Exhibition. Every year the school put on an exhibition which was attended by those with an interest in the school. In the surviving Barrett Street visitors' books are the names and cards of some of the guests who attended the exhibitions. Many of the visitors were prospective employers, prompting the Principal, Miss Cox, to record that in 1921 'over two hundred firms visited the private view of the annual exhibition'. By the mid-1930s the exhibition became a far more elaborate affair and included a dress show and displays of dance.

2 *Right.* The Prospectus for Barrett Street.

3   The Prospectus for Shoreditch.

The fashion industry in the West End of London, at the turn of the century, produced much of the luxurious and hand crafted clothing worn by women of the leisured classes. This was due to its unique location in the heart of the capital city, the centre for government, commerce, entertainment and culture. Many of the aristocracy and leading families maintained a house in this area and were usually in residence between April and August. This was when the London 'season' took place; a round of court presentations, balls, parties, cultural and sporting events. In addition, many affluent women travelled to the West End to obtain their clothes from exclusive dressmakers, fashion houses and smart department stores, whose workrooms made fashionable made-to-measure clothing.

This fashionable dress trade accounted for only part of the needle-trade industry in London which employed both men and women. Traditionally the men's bespoke tailoring trade, centred on Savile Row, employed men. Women found employment either in the ready-to-wear trade, centred on London's East End, or in the fashionable dressmaking and allied trades serving 'society' clientèle in the West End. This high-class trade was predominantly based around South Kensington, Mayfair, Oxford Street, Regent Street and the adjacent roads. Because of the specialised and high quality work required by the West End fashion trade, women working in this area had to be skilled artisans, the majority of whom were employed in the workrooms; cutting, decorating, making and fitting garments. The early needle-trade schools in London trained women for specialised high quality couture work which is summed up in a Board of Education report of 1924:

> they enabled girls to enter certain of the London trades which necessitated a high standard of skill, intelligence, initiative, originality and artistic perception in order that the standard of production required by the public may be maintained and a successful career for the individual assured.[1]

Advances in technology, for example the power-driven sewing machine and the widespread use of the multiple cutting band knife, meant that the factory-made ready-to-wear clothing industry was beginning to flourish in various parts of the country. This did not seem to affect the high-class trade in the West End of London; rather, the growth of the ready-to-wear market in the first half of the century appeared to co-exist comfortably with the high-class West End trade. The clothes made for women attending society events were made-to-measure creations in expensive materials which could not be mass produced. When Edward VII ascended the throne in 1901 court and society flourished and the old aristocracy was joined by the 'nouveaux riches', many of whom had obtained their wealth as a result of the industrial revolutions. Women in this leisured class were keen to display their wealth by way of luxurious clothes.

Before the introduction of needle-trade schools, girls were recruited from elementary schools to work as 'learners' in the exclusive court and society dressmakers' houses and smart department stores. Needlework was a compulsory part of the elementary school curriculum. However, the level of skills required by the exclusive West End trade went far beyond the basic skills taught in these schools.[2] Indentured apprenticeships were rarely given to women; training would be informal and depended on the willingness of the employer or experienced staff to devote time to training. As social reformers such as Henry Mayhew testified in the 19th century, the pay for girls working in the dress trade was low, and for the unskilled it was exceptionally low. Girls who were able to enter informal apprenticeships were taught the skills of the trade, which gave them greatly improved prospects of employment and enabled them to command higher wages. However, as Clementina Black pointed out in 1909, many girls were not able to take advantage of this opportunity and earned their living by 'trotting'—working for short periods, in the London 'season', learning whatever skills they could.[3] The skills they learned depended upon the work given to them and the garments the customers ordered. This system often called for long working hours, in poor conditions, for low pay and it provided little opportunity for their advancement. Rents in the capital were rising and employers were increasingly reluctant to train their staff. Many were employing skilled workers from the Continent. This meant that there was beginning to be a shortage of skilled British labour in the high class trade. In 1893, the Technical Education Board for London, under the chairmanship of Sidney Webb, had started to look at ways to maintain skill levels in a number of trades. It appointed a special committee to look at the technical instruction that was available to women. It concluded that Britain was lacking the type of training that was available in French *Ecoles Professionels*, some of which provided artistic and skilled training in the needle trades.[4] Increasingly, London's upper-class women were obtaining some of their clothes from Paris which had a thriving well established couture trade. As transport improved, this trade was growing and was seen to be a real threat to the high-class London trade.

It was against this background that the first girls' needle-trade school was founded at the Borough Polytechnic in 1904. It was intended only as an experiment and the girls were taught 'made to order' waistcoat making.[5] The experiment proved to be very successful and wages for the girls were better than average when they moved in employment because of their newly acquired skills. The experiment was extended the following year when upholstery, embroidery, ladies' tailoring and dressmaking courses were added to the Borough Polytechnic prospectus. Emulating this success, Shoreditch Technical Institute opened a girls' trade school in 1906, offering trade courses in dressmaking, embroidery and upholstery. Other needle-trade schools followed, including Barrett Street Trade School, which was founded in 1915 in an old elementary school at the back of Selfridges department store.[6] It offered courses in dressmaking, tailoring and hairdressing; embroidery was added a few years later. Clapham Trade School was founded in the 1920s. These schools were classed by the Board of Education as Junior Technical Schools. The courses were intended to provide training for students in one skilled trade similar to an indentured apprenticeship, together with physical and general education. As the trades in question were the needle trades, these schools were colloquially referred to as 'needle-trade schools'.

4 Barrett Street students on the roof of Selfridges in 1932. The school building, which is still part of the present college, is immediately behind the department store.

The London County Council [LCC], which assumed the responsibilities of the London School Board in 1903, had clear criteria for its girls' needle-trade schools. They were to provide the labour-intensive high-class dress trade with trained artisans and were intended to replace the informal apprenticeships that had existed in some of the more enlightened dress houses. Girls, who were generally referred to as students, came to the trade schools, usually after completing their elementary education at twelve to fourteen years of age. This was because young girls were considered to be the most adaptable at learning fine needle skills. The courses were vocational and lasted two years. For students attending the full-time course, training was organised like a typical LCC secondary school of the era. Attendance was for approximately 30 hours a week during term time. The students had the usual school holidays and were required to wear a school uniform. As an alternative to an apprenticeship the schools were not intended as preparation for university, higher technical education or commercial training.[7] Indeed, the schools' curricula were set-up in consultation with local industry to meet its requirements.

5 The Barrett Street student common room in the 1920s.

6 Mannequin parade staged for Barrett Street students by Mrs. Robert Mathis 'Poulain' of George Street, a society dressmaker in April 1924.

7 Miss Ethel Cox, English mistress at Shoreditch from 1911-5, and the first principal of Barrett Street. She held the post from 1915 until 1950. Miss Cox was 40 when this photograph was taken of her in a court gown she wore to be presented at the Court of George V in her capacity as Mayoress of Wandsworth. Miss Cox's father, a widower, was elected Mayor in 1929 and Miss Cox, his eldest daughter, acted as mayoress. Her silk dress was made by the students of Barrett Street to the strict court regulations issued by the Office of the Lord Chamberlain.

The curriculum was divided into one-third general education and two-thirds on the chosen trade subject. A central Needle-trades Consultative Committee, made up of leading members of the West End clothing trades' and employers' associations, met at County Hall [opposite the Houses of Parliament] to advise on the curriculum of all the London needle-trade schools. Thus much of the trade's requirements were included in the schools' curriculum. In addition, each school had its own consultative committees, made up of members of the local trade, to advise on individual trade subjects.

Shoreditch Girls Trade School was housed within the Shoreditch Institute, which ran other day and evening courses, including a teacher training course and trade courses for boys in bespoke tailoring and furniture making. The trade school was run in the same building as the Shoreditch Domestic Economy School, which trained girls for domestic service; both were housed in a separate block at the back of the main school. Although separate, the two schools were run under the same headmistress, a Miss H.J. Plowright. The First World War saw a decline in the numbers of girls wishing to enter domestic service, resulting in the school's closure in 1919, and the needle-trade school taking over its rooms.[8]

Whilst Shoreditch was situated in the East End of London, Barrett Street had the immediate advantage of being in the centre of the West End trade which it served. Miss Ethel Cox became the first headmistress, having previously been English mistress at Shoreditch School. Most of the girls who attended Shoreditch during this time came from North and North East of London; while, due to its West End location, the students of Barrett Street often had to travel.[9] Most junior students came directly from elementary schools and from a background where their parents were in semi-skilled and skilled trade occupations. Former students testify that many of the girls came from a Jewish background. [The tailoring and dressmaking trades in London during this period had large numbers of Jewish workers.] Barrett Street enrolment records for the 1920s, which give parental details, show that many of the girls came from families where the father had been killed in the First World War. The LCC recognised that it would have to award scholarships to help families to maintain their daughters while training. Scholarships were given on successful completion of an examination. They covered the fees and included a maintenance grant which varied according to family income. The first scholarships were only available to those students whose family income did not exceed £3 a week or £150 a year.[10] In 1910, 55 per cent of girls in trade schools received scholarships; this figure rose to 68 per cent in 1917 before dipping to 52 per cent in 1922.[11] In addition, the fees of a number of students were paid by charitable institutions.

In 1926, Barrett Street, in response to suggestions from the trade, started to take senior students aged 15 and above. Fewer scholarships were given to senior students. As a rule, junior school students started in the workrooms, although school records testify to many who rose rapidly in the trade. Most senior school students, who for the most part attended secondary, central, high and grammar schools, obtained jobs 'on the staff' as fitters, cutters, designer cutters, and designers. The courses ran for two years. Junior students could enrol on an accelerated senior course and complete it within a year.

Another feature of both the Shoreditch and Barrett Street schools was their programme of day release and evening classes for women already working in the needle trades. Barrett Street was particularly successful in attracting evening-class students because of its proximity to West End dressmakers, fashion houses and department stores; its prospectus stated that 'admission is restricted to those working in the trade'. Many former junior trade school students, who from financial restraint, were unable to attend the senior courses, carried on learning their trade in evening classes, enabling them to leave the workroom and to obtain jobs 'on the staff'.[12] Barrett Street also ran a part-time courses for 'Ladies Maids' in dressmaking and hairdressing.

8   Barrett Street pupils on a school visit in the 1930s.

Needle-trade schools were staffed both by academic staff and trade staff. The academic staff generally had academic qualifications; school records show many held degrees.[13] They were appointed by the head of the school and by members of the LCC. The trade staff of both Shoreditch and Barrett Street were not required to have teaching experience but had to have experience in a workroom. They were appointed by the trade school head and members of the schools' trade consultative committee. Most came to work at the schools direct from West End needle trades. To the newly appointed staff, working in a trade school offered better pay and working conditions. The appointment of trade staff with skills obtained from the clothing industry enabled the needle-trade schools to stay in close touch with the needs of the industry. Former students recall that, whilst most of their trade teachers were very efficient and adaptable, a few did not have teaching and organisational skills and were unreceptive to new ideas. Trade teachers were required to sit a practical examination at the interview. Records held at Barrett Street show that the position of trade teacher was very popular and there was strong competition for the posts.[14] Most of the three schools' art teachers received their training at art school and had worked in the needle trades. Barrett Street, for example, employed a part-time practising fashion artist. LCC records show that careful consideration was given to the appointment of physical exercise teachers, as it was recognised that women working in the needle trades were vulnerable to illnesses relating to or caused by the sedentary nature of their work. LCC Inspectors were always keen to ensure that needle-trade schools taught physical education using the latest methods. The inspection report for Barrett Street in 1936 commented that the physical education teachers 'provided good activity and postural training'.

9 Barrett Street students playing net ball. As with all schools of the 1920s and 1930s, great emphasis was placed on physical education. In common with many inner-city schools, Barrett Street had a caged games court on the roof. The cage and court still survive.

10 & 11 Barrett Street students using the equipment in the gymnasium. Badges were awarded for good performance.

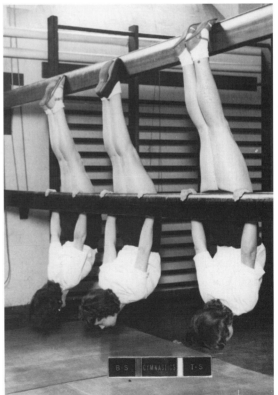

As students of Shoreditch and Barrett Street were trained to work in the West End trade all full-time junior trade courses finished in March. This coincided with the beginning of the London 'season', when the workrooms of fashion houses and the department stores were looking for extra staff. Most of the students obtained employment through personal recommendation, the trade teacher suggesting firms that would suit each student. Many prospective employers visited the schools' annual exhibition of work, which in the case of Barrett Street was always held in December and often hand-picked the students they wanted. This close relationship with the industry resulted in former students of London needle-trade schools of this period finding it relatively easy to gain employment. The Board of Education confirmed this in its 1923 inspection report for Shoreditch which stated that, 'out of a total of 751 girls who have completed the two year course by 1922, only seven have failed to take up the trades for which they were prepared and almost without exception had adequate reasons for'. A LCC inspection report on Barrett Street for 1936 also states that 'the demand for the services of girls training for the needle-trades in London Junior Technical Schools is much in excess of supply and this school is no exception'.

As well as the LCC scholarship examination, which a large majority of junior students took, both junior and senior students were required to attend an interview at the school of their choice, supported by a parent, guardian or teacher. The parents, or guardians, of girls in needle trades were expected to undertake that their daughters would enter the trade for which they were trained.

Former students of Barrett Street state that Miss Cox conducted interviews at Barrett Street in the absence of trade teachers. A number of girls from working-class backgrounds remember being struck by the refinement of the establishment, compared with their elementary school, and by the lady-like appearance of Miss Cox. Students remember being asked to show her their hands. One student remembers being told she would only be considered for a place if she stopped biting her nails suggesting that Miss Cox wanted 'lady-like', well cared-for hands. The more likely explanation was that the courses were practical and it was important that students had the use of all their fingers.

Junior students at trade schools spent 20 hours a week on their chosen trade subject and 10 hours on general subjects. These subjects were English with elocution, geography, history, mathematics and physical education. Trade French was later added to the curriculum. Senior students spent less time on general subjects. Board of Education Inspectors at this time were generally happy with the curriculum in general subjects, but many former students suggest that the work taught was of a very general nature.[15]

As all the LCC needle-trades schools had the same central Needle-trades Consultative Committee, their trade curricula were very similar. Each trade class contained sixteen to twenty students; former students recall that the classes were very relaxed and no pressure was placed on them to build-up the output of their work to the speed that the trade would eventually require. Emphasis was placed on the learning of skills correctly to a high standard.

Training in the dressmaking, embroidery and tailoring classes in all three schools consisted of learning the stitches and techniques required by the high-class couture trade. In the dressmaking classes, samplers would be worked on in a variety of fabrics ranging from fine silk to wool, before proceeding to the making of garments. Photographs of samplers done by Mary Wildman, a junior school student at Barrett Street, are included

12 An English class at Clapham Trade School in 1930.

in this book's second section [see pages 123-128]. Her samples include hand-rolled hems, hand button holes, fine pin tucks, pleats and a number of seams and seam finishes, and they show the high standard of hand-work which was required by the West End trade. Senior school students were also required to make samples but spent less time on general subjects, receiving instruction instead in pattern making and cutting. Junior trade students were taught fashion sketching in the art class but no pattern-cutting was attempted.

The junior dressmaking students at Barrett Street would learn some pattern cutting by watching the teacher, working from a sketch, and model the garment they were to make on-the-stand using a soft cotton fabric. Seams were then marked and a pattern was made. This pattern was not a standard size, but was made to the client's exact measurements. Members of staff and associates of the school acted as clients and chose the design and material they wanted. One former student recalls the dress-stands that were padded to match the measurements of staff. Senior students designed, cut, and made garments of their choice for the annual fashion show using material donated by the local trade. It is these garments that are recalled in the photographs in the second part of this book which formed the final work of the students for display to future employers. During the 1920s and 1930s junior dressmaking students made only three garments which were chosen by the trade teacher to reflect the individual's competence. All were made in the couture manner, using techniques learned through preparing samples. In the final term an interview outfit was made by junior trade students when a commercial paper pattern was used. This was, according to former students, the only time a pattern was used. Although art training was given to all students, junior students were trained to carry out garment-making in the workroom. Senior students spent more time in the art studio learning commercial design skills.

Trade embroidery students were taught both hand and machine embroidery. As with dressmaking students, girls studying embroidery started their course with stitching practice on a variety of different weights and fabrics before using both the machine and a hand frame. Students then went on to apply these skills to the decoration of garments. As the photographs show, braiding, fringing, metal thread and beading work were also taught. The consultative committees monitored the curriculum closely. In the late 1920s there was a shortage of employment in the London embroidery trade. This was due to the drop in demand for highly decorative and evening and court wear in favour of simpler, but technically complex body moulding styles with less surface decoration. In response the LCC higher education sub-committee, on the recommendation of the Needle-trades Consultative Committee's, supplemented nine hours' embroidery instruction for trade dressmaking.[16]

During the 1930s as fashion and women's lives were changing so the West End clothing industry changed. The number of court and society dressmakers making elaborately decorated court and evening gowns dropped. Women from all sections of society were beginning to demand more practical clothes. Although Barrett Street continued to train students in couturier skills, new courses were introduced at Shoreditch. In 1927, Shoreditch, following a Board of Education and Ministry of Labour suggestion, started training women in the production of men's ready-made work clothing. This course was run alongside the established dress and embroidery courses.

It can be seen that London needle-trade schools owe much of their success to the close working relationship between the LCC and the local needle trades. Although the training, particularly in the junior sections of the school, was very broad, students obtained a good introduction to the craft. In an industry that used much casual labour and traditionally paid low wages, there is every evidence that needle-trade students were more likely to find regular and secure employment that was paid above average wages. The main reason given at the time for this high level of employment was the systematic training provided by the schools. Girls that entered the trade with no formal training often did the same type of work throughout their working lives and were given little opportunity to expand their skills. Trade-school students had learnt a range of techniques and were therefore adaptable. A particular strength of Barrett Street was the way it persuaded former students to continue their study at evening class, thereby increasing their opportunities for advancement in the trade. Former junior students who had started work in workrooms often obtained staff positions by studying at evening class.

As the photographs show, the standard of work in all three trade schools was very high. Although the photographic collections recall some interesting designs, it could be argued that they were commercial rather than at the very leading edge of fashion. This could be explained by the close relationship the schools had with the trade. The West End clothing trade in London was concerned with making garments for society occasions. Whilst many women would have required the latest fashions, equally there were those who wanted very high quality well-made conservative clothes. Both Shoreditch and Barrett Street were linked with a trade that was also producing court and society wear, not generally known for pioneering designs. Many of the students would go on to make court wear which required the technical skills of highly trained embroidresses, dressmakers and tailoresses who could produce clothes to the requirements of court and society etiquette.

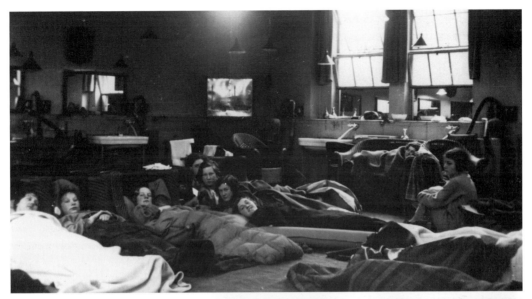

13 Barrett Street pupils sleeping on the floor of a classroom the night before George VI was crowned. In May 1937, many children from LCC schools watched the coronation procession from the Victoria Embankment. To be ready on time the selected group spent the previous night in the school. Other pupils attended the youth rally at the Albert Hall and the service at Westminster Hall to mark the occasion. Due to the school's proximity to the procession route, a number of members of staff and invited guests watched the procession from the roof and upper windows of the school's buildings.

14 Cover of a scrapbook compiled by pupils to describe their experiences as evacuees. During the Second World War most inner-city school children were evacuated to safer areas. Shoreditch pupils were sent to High Wycombe where the Board of Education rented 'The Limes' as a temporary school building.

Many of London's court and society fashion houses and exclusive stores, had representatives that served both the central and schools' Needle-trades Consultative Committees. Mrs. Handley-Seymour, Revilles, Liberty's, Jays, Harvey Nichols, Selfridges, Marshall and Snelgrove all had representatives advising on the curriculum. Thoughout the 1920s and early 1930s both Queen Mary and the Duchess of York [later Queen Elizabeth] bought clothes from Mrs. Handley-Seymour and Revilles and occasionally from the workrooms of the exclusive London stores. Many 'society' ladies followed suit. These establishments were famed for their painstaking workmanship and the elaborate decorations on their court wear rather than for their creative and original flair. Shoreditch, Barrett Street and Clapham trade schools in this era trained for this exclusive market, which employed its students and required traditional couture techniques and high standards.

15 Shoreditch pupils helped to gather the harvest whilst staying at High Wycombe.

16 Barrett Street Trade School had a collection of flags which were used on ceremonial occasions such as Empire Day. This photograph, taken in Maidenhead, to where the school was evacuated, shows the flags being used in the civic procession to mark the start of the town's peace celebration in 1945. This was the last occasion on which the flags were used.

During the Second World War, due to labour and material shortages, many firms in the luxury market were forced to curtail their output further: many closed altogether. Firms could only produce elaborate creations for the export market. The Board of Trade encouraged mass produced 'conveyor-belt' clothing for the home market. After the war, due to changes in the education system and the influence of the Design Council which was closely connected with the art schools' training for the fashion industry, the old established firms began to lose their influences. The central Needle-trades Consultative Committee was disbanded. Barrett Street, due to its central West End location, continued to service the exclusive trade. Shoreditch, which had amalgamated with Clapham in March 1940 following the retirement of its principal Miss K. A. Corner, greatly expanded its courses for the ready-to-wear market. The following photographs are unique, representing a past era made possible by the working relationship between LCC trade schools and the West End couture trade.

Footnotes

1. 'Report of H.M. Inspectors on Junior Technical Education given in London Trade Schools for Girls for the period ending 31 July 1924', p.1.
2. 'The Board of Education Report on the Teaching of Needlework in Public Elementary Schools' [1912] opening paragraph states that schools should 'ensure every girl can cut out, make and keep in repair the ordinary garments she is likely to require in her own home'. The needle skills required by the exclusive West End trade went far beyond this.
3. Black, C. and Meyer, C., *The Makers of our Clothes*, Duckworth [1909] p.12.
4. Additional information can be obtained in *Trade Schools on the Continent*, HMSO [Industry Series No. 11, 1930].
5. *Trade and Domestic Training for Girls*, HMSO [1929] p.5.
6. *Reports of Board of Education for 1915/16*, H.M.S.O.
7. *Hadow Report on the Education of the Adolescent*, Appendices, HMSO [1926] p. 271.
8. 'Short History of the Secondary Technical School attached to Shoreditch College for the Garment Trades' prepared by Second Year Dressmakers and Tailors [1953]. Unpublished, p.6. London College of Fashion Archive.
9. Enrolment registers Barrett Street Trade School 1915-1936. London College of Fashion Archive.
10. *The Technical Education Board of London County Council Pocket Book* [Jan.1904] p.180.
11. 'Report of H.M. Inspectors on Junior Technical Education given in London Trade Schools for Girls for the period ending 31 July 1924', p.13.
12. Barrett Street Prospectuses 1916-1939 and oral history interviews.
13. The Shoreditch Institute Girls Trade School Staff Register [1906-1920]. London College of Fashion Archive.
14. Minute Book for Barrett Street Trade School Consultative Committee Staff Sub Committee [1915-1930]. London College of Fashion Archive.
15. 'Report of an Inspection of LCC Barrett Street Trade School by LCC Higher Education Sub Committee' [November 1936].
16. Metropolitan Archives EO/HFE/6/17. Meeting of Needle-trades Consultative Committee at County Hall, 12 December 1929.

THE STUDENTS' WORK

When Miss Ethel Cox became Principal of the Barrett Street Trade School she actively encouraged the preservation of photographs, printed material and other ephemera that related to the school. She also kept a series of personal scrapbooks. In addition some of the student and staff records have survived. These collections are now housed in the London College of Fashion Archive. Over the years, further items have been added to the archive and currently continue to be collected by the college's Special Collections Librarian. The majority of the following photographs come from this unique collection.

Most of the photographs in the college archive that relate to Shoreditch are of Shoreditch College for the Garment Trades, the successor to Shoreditch Institute Girls Trade School. These photographs were taken after 1949 when Mrs. Dorothy Glasswell was principal and Mr. William Orange was vice principal. They were added to the archive together with some early written records after 1961, when the college merged with Barrett Street. As they do not relate to the early period they have not been included in this selection. Fortunately, early photographs of Shoreditch Institute Girls Trade School and Clapham Trade School taken by the LCC have been preserved in the Metropolitan Archives photographic collection.

Whilst some of the photographs published in the following selection have been preserved with their original documentation, most were preserved without accompanying details. Former students have been able to recall some details, however, but many photographs in the archive still remain without documentation. Despite this, The London College of Fashion photographs provide a fascinating insight into a vocational college adapting to meet the demands of the clothing industry, the education authorities and the needs of the pupils and students attending the courses. The early photographs, a selection of which is printed in this book, provide visual information about the methods employed to teach girls and women the professional skills needed to earn a living in the high-class London needle trades. The finished garments in the following photographs, all made by the students, are individual creations in the fashionable styles of the period. Many of the photographs are of court and evening wear reflecting the demand at the time for pupils and students who had the skills to make these elaborate hand-crafted gowns. Most of the photographs, which are arranged chronologically, show the change in women's fashionable dress over the first half of this century.

All the mannequins [the term used during this period for models] came from the college's students. This accounts for the occasional photograph of adolescent girls in clothes more suited to the mature figure. However, most of the mannequins display the clothes with great aplomb reflecting oral history evidence of women, with couture dressmaking and tailoring skills, displaying a great deal of style. This was due to the skills they learned at the needle-trade schools, enabling them not only to make stylish clothes for themselves, but also, most importantly, to earn a living.

17 The dressmaking class at the Shoreditch Technical Institute, Girls Trade School in 1907, the year after the School opened. Although needlework had been taught to girls in schools long before this date, it had been one of the subjects for domestic instruction which focused on needle-skills required for the home. As a trade school, Shoreditch taught the commercial needle skills needed by a skilled artisan to earn a living. The women trade teachers at this time were not required to have had any form of teacher training but were expected to have had considerable experience working in the needle trades.

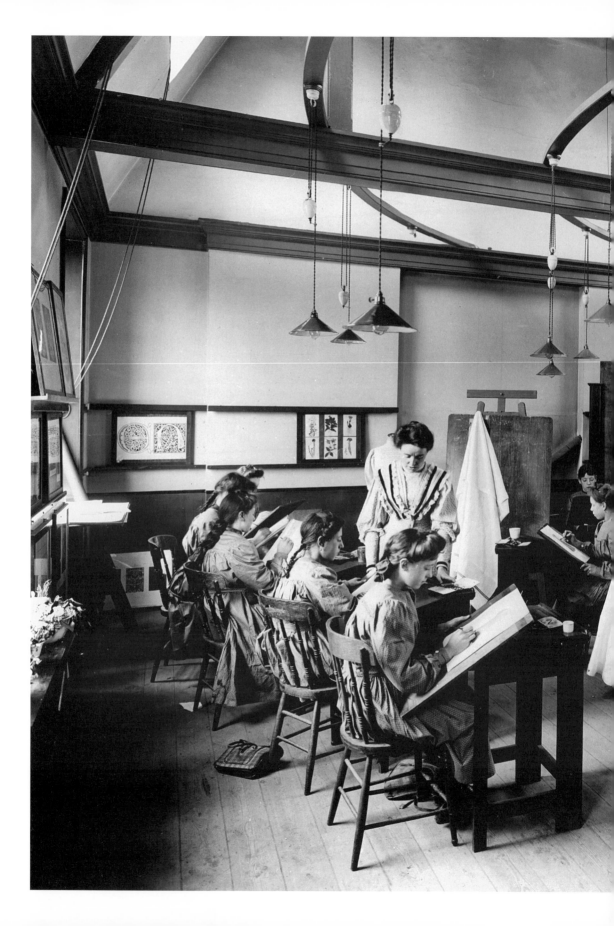

18 The art class at Shoreditch in 1907 shows pupils receiving instruction in fashion sketching. The aim of the LCC needle-trade schools was to train girls to be creative artisans as well as skilled technicians. Pupils were expected not only to sketch finished garments but to study the drape of the fabrics they were working with and accurately reflect their properties in the finished sketches.

19-21 This display shows examples of the pupils' completed work which was mounted in the costume room at Shoreditch soon after the school opened. The garments show the wide range of fine hand- and machine-skills the girls learned. Although the school was situated in north-east London, which had a thriving wholesale clothing trade, the skills the pupils were learning were those required by the 'high class' trade. After training, the majority of the girls found employment in the workrooms of the exclusive dressmakers, fashion houses and department stores in London's West End. The pupils' work shows an interesting mix of costume styles which co-existed at this time. The blouse in the foreground of Fig. 19 is reminiscent of the 'S' line style of the turn of the century which required the wearer to achieve the shape using heavily boned corsets. The dresses on the stands have a slightly straighter silhouette and the raised waistline of the directoire revival. The cotton day dress in Figs. 19 and 21 is decorated with chemical lace.

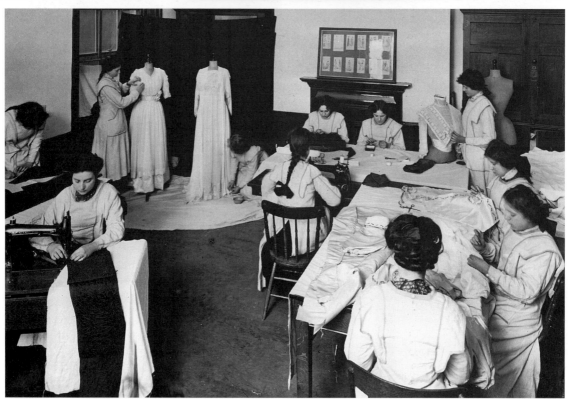

22 *Left.* Examples of embroidery for dress and light upholstery done by pupils on the embroidery and upholstery courses that were shown in the same display as the garments on the previous display.

23 *Below left.* Pupils learning dressmaking techniques at Shoreditch, *c*.1911. To protect the garments from soiling, tables are covered and the pupils wear overalls. Although sewing machines were used in exclusive dress houses of this period, their use was mainly confined to seams and decorative work. Fine hand-sewing techniques were still used extensively. This class has only two sewing machines [treadle] in use.

24 *Below.* The dressmaking class at Shoreditch, *c*.1912. The dress stand in the photograph has a very pronounced waist which many women hoped to achieve, with the help of corsets, at the turn of the century. The dress stands in subsequent photographs have less pronounced waists, reflecting later less curvaceous and freer styles.

25 & 26   *Above and above right.* Barrett Street Trade School opened in 1915, during the First World War. These two photographs show pupils at work in the tailoring and dressmaking classes, the two needle trades offered when the school opened. The sewing machine being used in the tailoring class is made by the Singer Sewing Machine Company. Singer sewing machines had been used by girls in London schools from the 1890s onwards. During the last quarter of the 19th century the company was actively exploring new markets for their products. Promoting their product to needle-trade schools was seen as a good way of securing future custom. Attractive discounts and after-sales care and service were therefore offered to the LCC. Examples of work done by both Barrett Street and Shoreditch pupils appeared in *Red Review*, the Singer magazine. The dress on the dress stand in Fig. 26 illustrates the move towards more practical and comfortable styles of clothes for women.

27   *Right.* Pupils drawing in the art studio at Barrett Street, 1915. Fashion illustrations from contemporary trade periodicals were prominently displayed on the walls of both the art and trade rooms. This photograph was used alongside photographs of the trade classrooms in the 1916 prospectus.

28 Unfortunately we have no details about the provenance of this photograph except that it comes from the Barrett Street collection and was probably taken during the First World War. The school operated a prefect system and one of the pupils dressed in trade overalls is wearing her prefect's badge. To help protect the school's oak flooring Miss Cox insisted that all junior trade pupils should wear plimsolls whilst indoors.

Unless otherwise stated the following photographs show the work of Barrett Street Trade School. From about 1920, School and LCC records generally refer to the girls and women who attended needle-trade schools as students. Junior and senior school students wore school uniform and were aged between twelve and seventeen. Women who attended the evening classes and day release classes were older.

29 A student working on an evening gown with an over dress and lace bodice, c.1919.

30 Velvet evening gown with train, and fashionable high waist of the directoire revival, c.1919.

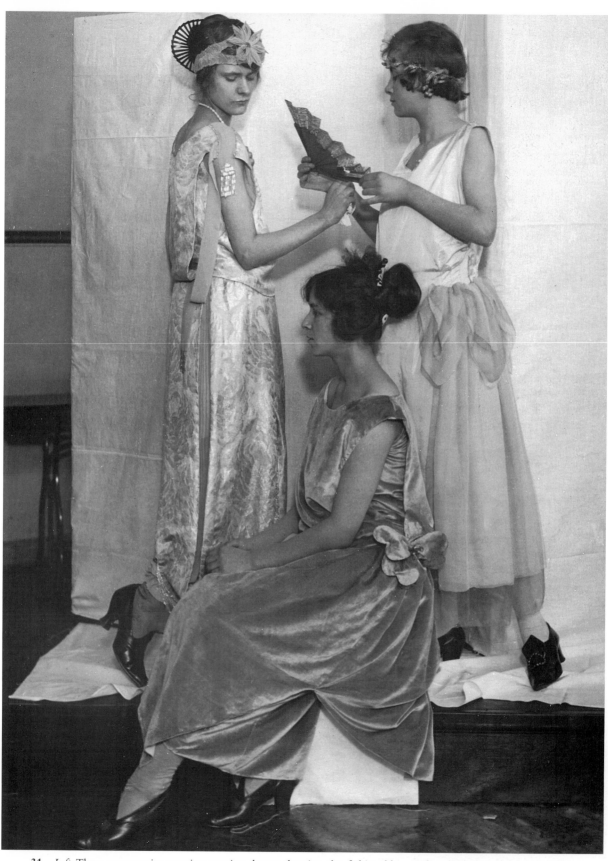

31 *Left*. Three mannequins wearing evening dresses showing the fashionable waistline beginning to drop, *c*.1922.

32 Two dresses made by students, *c.*1922. As hem lines started to rise stockings became more noticeable. Although seamed stockings were available at this time, many women still wore circular-knit stockings which, as this photograph shows, did not give a smooth and close fit around the ankle.

33 Evening dress, short with puffed sleeves and scalloped hem. The student mannequin carries a long string of beads which were a popular accessory in this era, *c.*1922.

34 Dress with fine pin tucks on the skirt, *c.*1923.

35 The discoveries in the tomb of Tutankhamen in 1922 had a profound effect on the decorative arts, including dress. This day dress with an asymmetrical design on the sleeve is inspired by Egyptian hieroglyphs.

36 Due to the demand by the West End needle trades for women with trade embroidery skills, Barrett Street introduced an embroidery course in 1917. This photograph is of students aged between twelve and fifteen learning both hand- and machine-embroidery skills. The Cornely machines being used were very popular in the embroidery trade at this time. They were regarded as one of the most versatile embroidery machines on the market because of the number of stitches and different effects produced on fabrics ranging from fine silk to heavy woollens.

37 Women attending evening classes in dressmaking. This photograph, and the one on the facing page, appeared in the school prospectus in 1924. Barrett Street ran both 'day release' and evening classes for women working in the West End trade who wanted to improve their trade skills. Alongside trade classes women were encouraged to take art or an academic subject. These included French, dramatic literature, a favourite of Miss Cox's, and elocution. As it was recognised that women who worked continuously over a number of years in the needle trades were prone to health problems, women attending the trade classes were allowed 'subject to the approval of the principal' to attend the physical exercise class at no extra cost.

38 An evening art class, showing the student mannequin from the previous photograph. Classes started at seven o'clock and because most of the students attended classes directly from work, a rest room and food was provided. Unlike full-time students, women attending day release and evening classes were not required to wear a uniform. There were, in addition to the LCC Needle-trades School, a number of privately run schools in London offering similar courses. However, most of them did not enjoy the close association with the trade that the LCC Needle-trades School had fostered and generally they also charged higher fees.

39 & 40 Front and back view of an embroidered evening gown, *c.*1923. The mannequin is holding a presentation fan.

41 & 42 Two photographs of sleeveless evening dresses made in 1924 showing the fashionable tubular silhouette straight shape with the low waist and multi-level skirt. The long matching scarf, fur trimmings and arm bangle are typical of the period. The dress in the centre of the group of three appears in Fig. 37.

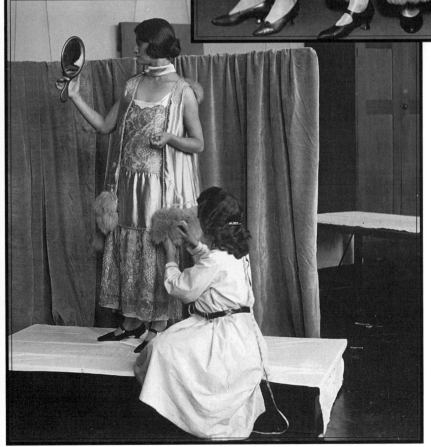

43 *Far left*. Accordion pleated day dress and suit worn with a cloche hat, *c*.1923–4. Although the position of the waist on women's garments was gradually dropped in the first half of the 1920s, fashionable skirt lengths for day wear fluctuated before finally settling on the knee.

44 *Left*. Formal dresses, *c*.1923–4. Scalloped and uneven hems were used on many formal and evening dresses of the period.

45 *Below left*. A dressmaking class, *c*.1924. The dress in Fig. 46 is being worked on by the student on the right side of the front table.

46 *Right*. This dress with puffed sleeves, horizontal tucks and a straight mid-calf hem, worn by a prepubescent student mannequin, does not convey the long tubular lines that were typically featured in the fashionable magazines of the time, *c*.1924.

47 *Left.* A student having her hair dressed, *c.*1925.

48 & 49 *Below left and right.* A number of the graduates of Barrett Street in the 1920s and '30s remember the many fine fabrics that were used to make the garments for the annual exhibition of work. Miss Cox and the trade staff of the school enjoyed a close working relationship with many West End firms, some of whom donated the materials for student use. Many of the girls either went to work or were working for these firms, and attended evening or day release courses. During the Second World War, due to government restrictions on the supply of material, this practice stopped. Many of the garments in this selection of photographs were made with fabrics obtained this way. This photograph of three evening dresses made in 1924 shows the skills of the dressmaking and embroidery students. The dress on the far left in fig. 48 and 49, see below, is made of silk georgette with hand figgoted inserts and has an elaborate draped skirt with uneven hem. The dress in the centre is made of gold tissue and black lace and the dress on the right is of black beaute and wine coloured georgette with a black beaded detail on the back.

50 & 51 Cloak made with insertions from a Chinese embroidered shawl, *c.*1924. Similar shawls were sold in great numbers at Liberty's department store. Mr. F. Henley of Liberty's was for a number of years chairman of Barrett Street School Needle-trades Consultative Committee and the store employed a number of the school's students in the workroom of their costume department.

52 Barrett Street student with a selection of the work done in the junior school. Samplers, containing a selection of techniques and stitches used in the West End needle trade at the time, were made by students before they went on to make complete garments. The work in the photograph formed part of an exhibition held at the London Day Training College, Southampton Row in 1927 to show the collective work of the London needle-trade schools. Apart from doing samples and making garments from trade donations of material, the students learnt their trade by making garments mainly for members of the staff. These commissions were to the requirements of the individual teacher and rarely appeared in photographs or the annual exhibition of work.

53-55 Samplers similar to those in Fig. 52 produced by first-year junior trade students in 1936 and 1937.

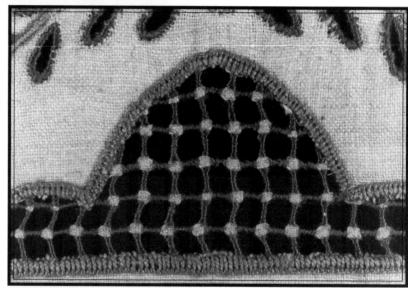

56 Young student modelling dress, *c.*1926.

57 Smoking jacket and two sleeveless dinner suits designed, embroidered and made by senior school students, *c.*1926-27. Oriental patterns, which were undergoing a strong revival at the time, were also used on decorative household items. This photograph shows clearly the straight lines of the 1920s, the fashion for short hair, and the expanse of leg, encased in glossy stockings, that the 'fashionable' were revealing. These stockings might be rayon which was beginning to be widely used as a cheap alternative to silk and contrast very sharply to the hard wearing lisle stockings worn by the full-time day students.

58 *Left.* The ladies' tailoring room at Barrett Street which was photographed for the 1927-8 school prospectus. Former students of the school recollected class sizes of between sixteen and twenty, so this class appears to be large. The students are learning to make bespoke tailored garments. These garments were individually made to the wearer's measurements. The outer fabric was shaped and moulded with special supporting inner fabrics. This required the use of specialised hand stitching. The room is therefore laid out predominantly for hand work with small sewing equipment kept in the centre of the table. Wooden foot rests are provided for the feet.

59 *Below left.* Evening-class students learning tailoring skills, *c.*1928. One of the reasons why Barrett Street was able to run so many evening classes was its central location, which made it easier for women already working in the West End needle trades to attend the courses.

60 *Below.* The evening class in advanced dressmaking skills held in the mid-1920s. Many women working as junior seamstresses or hands in the West End trade had little opportunity to further their dressmaking skills in a commercial workroom. Former junior seamstresses, with no formal training, tell of some workrooms giving them simple tasks and no opportunities to learn new skills. Evening classes gave these women the opportunity to learn new skills and thereby increase their promotion prospects. Former full-time junior trade students were also encouraged to attend classes to learn skills such as pattern-cutting, which was not taught on the junior trade course.

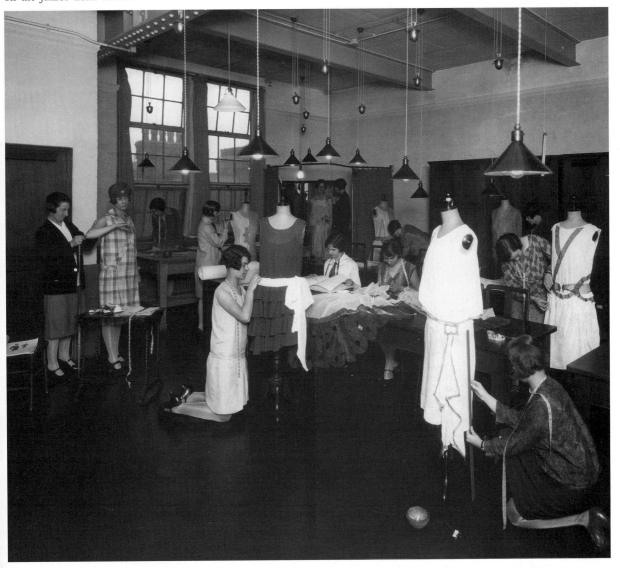

61 *Left*. Two evening dresses and a display of student work, *c*.1926–27. Shiny fabrics and light-reflecting embroidery were very popular at this time.

62 *Below*. Embroidery trade students of the 1920s with samples of their work. Embroidery on the dress was usually carried out before the material was cut and made up. Frames were used to keep the material taut, while it was being stitched.

63 *Right*. As garment making is a three-dimensional craft most of the students' work was carried out on the stand. This enabled the maker to see construction faults more readily and to visualise the finished result. The strongly textured embroidery on this garment is in an art deco style which, like many styles used in the decoration of dress, was applied to other media.

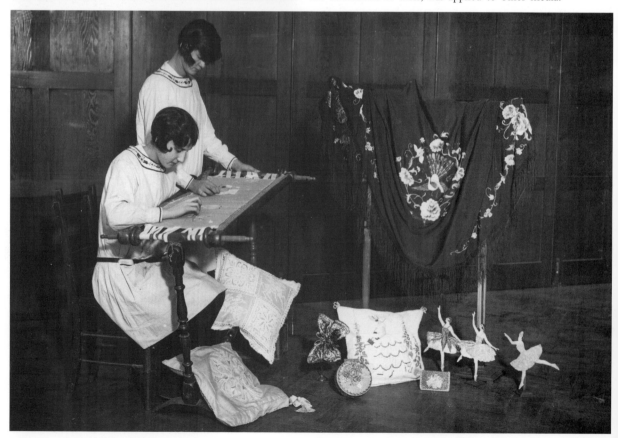

64 *Above left*. A typical sleeveless, dropped-waist evening dress of the mid-1920s, with an elaborate sash.

65 *Above right*. Formal silk dress, *c.*1928, with decorative shoulder detail and typical uneven hem.

66 *Top right*. The art studio at Barrett Street in 1928. On the walls of the studio are drawings that the students used when studying historical costume. Studying changes in the design, construction and decoration of historical dress was considered an important design and technical resource, and this subject therefore formed an integral part of all the courses at the school. The heavily embroidered court gown which also appears in Fig. 87 is very typical of the work that was being produced by embroidery students at the time.

67 *Bottom right*. Students learning embroidery skills at Barrett Street in the late 1920s. It was recognised that the skills needed by the West End clothing industry were constantly altering due to changes in fashion. During this era the embroidery trade had to adapt to the many changes in decorative styles which required different techniques. Students who enrolled for the trade embroidery courses were taught a broad range of commercially used hand- and machine-skills.

68 Students working on embroidery at Barrett Street in the late 1920s. Design skills were developed in the art studio. The embroidery course at Barrett Street was held in high regard by the exclusive dress houses and leading stores, who required women to embroider evening wear for high society functions and social events. The trade teachers themselves had often attended a trade school as well as working in the trade. Miss Shunn, later Mrs. Beck, one of the longest serving needle embroidery trade teachers at Barrett Street, attended Borough Polytechnic before working for a leading court dressmaker.

All students that enrolled learnt a branch of the trade such as tailoring, dressmaking or embroidery. However, they were also taught elements of the other trades. In addition, the embroidery students were required to spend two hours a week learning dressmaking. This was sharply increased at the end of the 1920s when the demand for highly embroidered garments fell. This gave the students the skill to work as dressmakers if they could not obtain work in the embroidery trade.

69–72 Some of the orient-inspired embroidered cocktail outfits and evening coats that were made by the embroidery trade students in the late 1920s. Fig. 70 appears on the stand in Fig. 67.

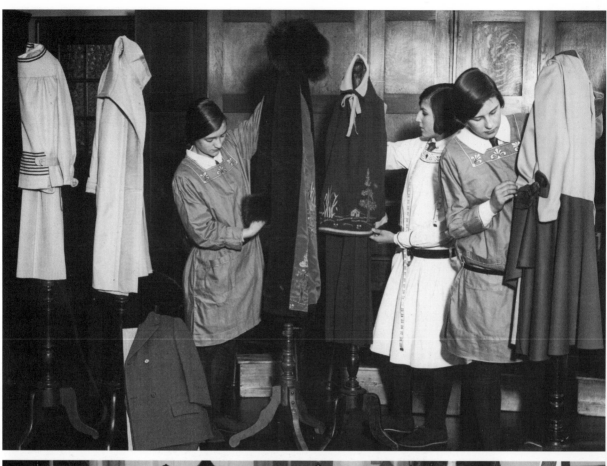

73 *Above left*. Up until the 1930s, when trade overalls were gradually replaced by a wrap round style, Barrett Street had different overall styles for the different needle trades. The tailoresses wore square-necked blue overalls, while the dressmakers and embroideresses wore off-white square- and round-necked overalls respectively.

74 *Left*. Students putting the finishing touches to embroidered gowns, *c*.1928. The suit on the left appears in Fig. 72.

75 *Above*. Three student mannequins displaying the work of dressmaking and embroidery students, *c*.1929. The evening gown on the right with the handkerchief hem is in georgette and embroidered with gold braid. The shawl worn over the top of this gown is described in the school's press release as a fashionable coatee.

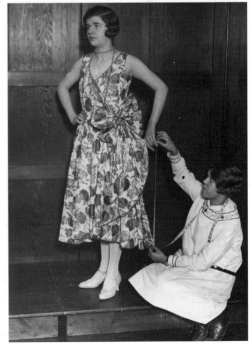

76 *Right*. Students putting the final touches to the printed day dress that appears in the previous photograph.

77 Children dressed in costumes made by Barrett Street students for the 1928 Mayor of London's Fancy Dress Ball. The child on the left with the cat is dressed as Dick Whittington.

78 Three evening outfits in the late 1920s. The centre dress shows a move towards the end of very tubular lines and the cape on the left has a large fur collar. As the photographs for this era show, fur was widely used to trim evening coats and capes.

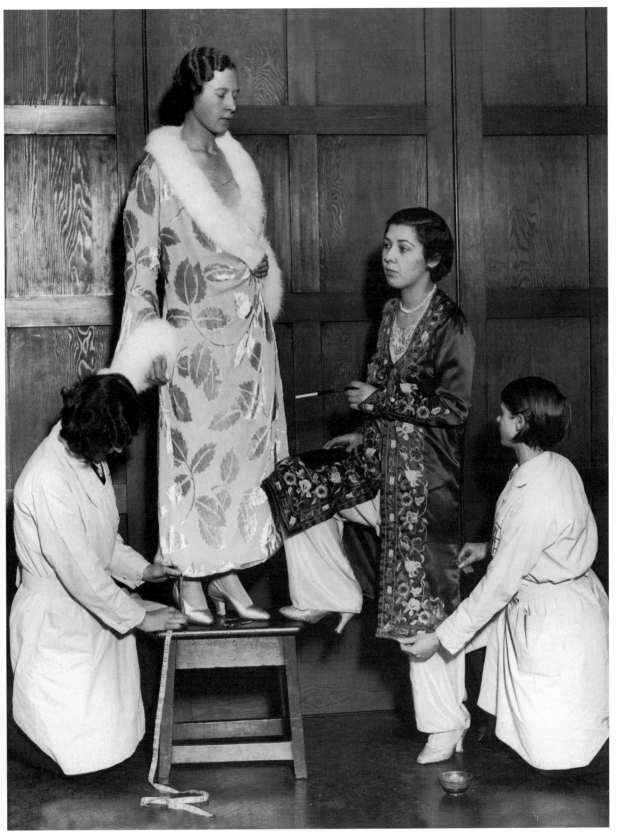

79 Evening clothes made by students in the late 1920s. From the 1920s trousers began to be accepted into mainstream fashion and were usually for informal wear. This photograph shows trousers being worn as part of a cocktail outfit.

80 *Left.* A display of students' work carried out in the mid-1920s including an evening bag.

81 *Below left.* Pupils working on two dresses, *c.*1930. This photograph highlights the intermix of styles that often co-existed. Although the dress on the right has hip-line seaming the belt is positioned around the natural position of the waistline while the dress on the left has no natural waistline detail bodice and hip-line embroidery detail.

82 *Below.* Evening dress made in the late 1920s.

83 Fortunately the school issued a press release which accompanied this photograph, which is preserved in the archive. It states that the frock is made of green spangled net and was designed and made by Miss Joan Fletcher who was 16 at the time. The embossed velvet evening cloak was designed and made by a 17-year-old student, Miss Phyllis Woodhead. Both were students at Barrett Street in 1929-30.

84 Tailored coats made by students in the late 1920s. The coat on the right of the picture has an embroidered lining showing the attention to detail that was demanded by the 'high-class trade'. The school blouse and tie, worn by junior and senior students is clearly visible under the blue trade overalls. The uniform consisted of a white blouse, tie, navy blue tunic, black stockings and knickers and a hat. The rules were relaxed slightly during the Second World War when rationing made strict adherence difficult and the uniform was dropped altogether when the school became a technical college after 1945.

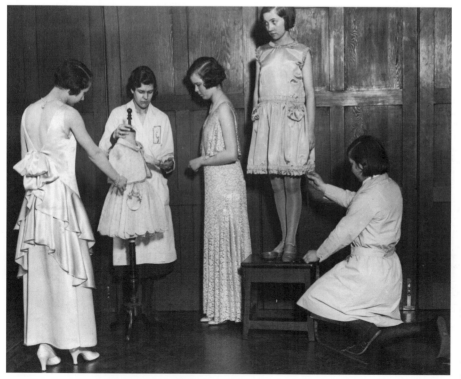

85 Long evening dresses and children's garments, *c.*1930. The students of Barrett Street frequently made children's garments and commissions for children's wear were generally given by LCC officials and the governors of the school.

86 Evening dress. This photograph, taken in the entrance hall of Barrett Street in 1930, shows the closer body fit which is associated with the 1930s; the waistline at its natural level and the hemline at ankle length.

87-89 Court gowns of the 1920s. Ever since the ruling monarch held formal courts, the women who attended them wore the most expensive clothing they could afford, in order to display their social standing. Over the years a court dress developed, which was far more decorative and elaborate than the clothing worn outside the court. By the end of the mid-1920s a thriving business had been built up by the leading West End dressmakers, fashion houses and department stores supplying court gowns and accessories. Social etiquette deemed it desirable for women who took part in London's society events to be presented at court. Formal presentations were dropped during the First World War but were resumed again in 1922 when an increasing number of women were presented. This led to extra demand for skilled workers who could design, embroider and make the formal gowns and trains. During this period Barrett Street trained many of the women who made these elaborate creations. The London College of Fashion has a number of photographs of court gowns made by its students while they were training. It was important that the students were familiar with the regulations pertaining to court wear: court gowns of the inter-war period generally followed the same line as fashionable evening dress with the addition of a prescribed head-dress, veil and feathers. The 1937 edition of *Dress Worn at Court* states that 'trains should not exceed 2 yards and the veil held in place by three white feathers mounted as a Prince of Wales Plume and should be no longer than 45 inches'. Although white was the preferred colour for debutantes, coloured gowns were permitted. Black was worn for mourning. Court gowns, without their trains, were often reused for formal evening wear.

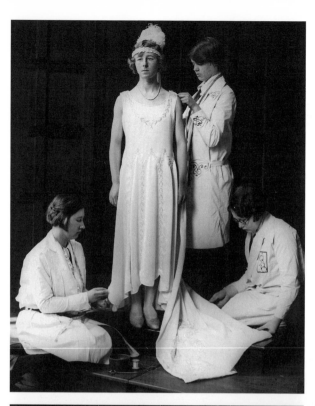

90 & 91 *Left and below left*. Photographs of two court presentation gowns and trains designed, embroidered and made by Barrett Street students. From the late 1920s through to the 1940s, just after the beginning of the Second World War, the prospectus for Barrett Street always included a photograph of a court gown made by its students, indicating the importance given in training for making formal court wear.

92 *Below right*. Back view of a court gown, showing the elaborate embroidery worked on the train. The head-dress and veil have been moved to one side to show the embroidered detail on the train. The large ostrich feather fans held by the mannequin were known as presentation fans.

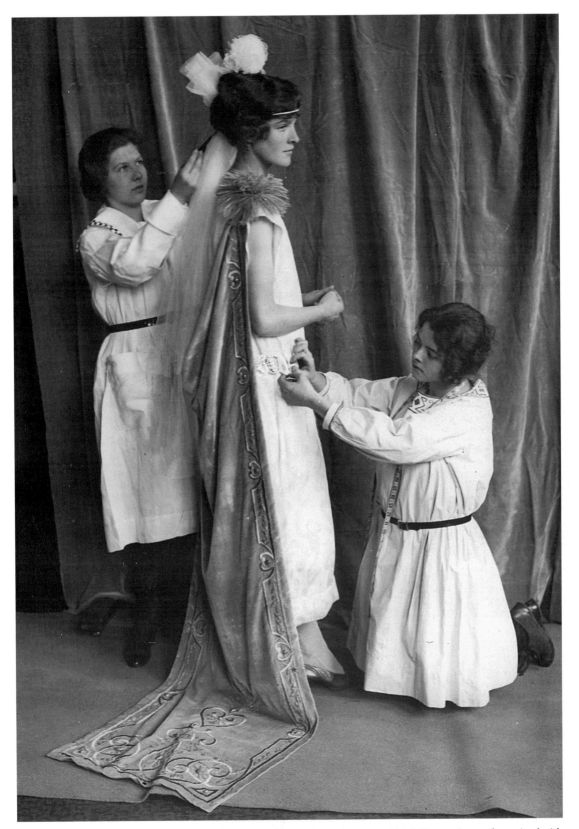

93 Finishing touches being made to a court dress and embroidered train, *c.*1924–5. Barrett Street also trained girls to work in the hairdressing and beauty trade. Before being photographed, the mannequins had their hair styled by hairdressing students.

94 & 95 *Left and below*. Barrett Street also ran courses in hairdressing which included instruction in beauty therapy. Many former hairdressing pupils would have worked in the West End, preparing women's hair for society events. These two photographs show student mannequins being prepared for the dress parade.

96 *Above right*. Because of its position in the heart of the West End, Barrett Street developed very successful lectures and practical courses for salesmen and women in West End stores. The school's consultative committee, in particular Mr. Herbert Kay, then secretary of the London employers' association, was instrumental in the development of these courses. Many eminent people gave lectures including Willett Cunnington, the well known fashion historian, and Alison Settle, fashion journalist and editor of *Vogue* during the 1930s. These lectures were later deemed by the LCC to be outside the scope of Barrett Street Trade School and the majority were transferred to the College for Distributive Trades. This photograph shows Mrs. Hall, head of the embroidery department at Barrett Street, teaching embroidery techniques to shop assistants from the needle-work departments of large stores. This course ran one evening a week for three terms, to which were sent sales assistants from Harrods, Peter Jones, D.H. Evans, Swan and Edgar, Bourne and Hollingsworth and Selfridges.

97 *Below right*. Clapham Trade School ran a very successful millinery course. This photograph shows students working in the millinery room in the late 1920s.

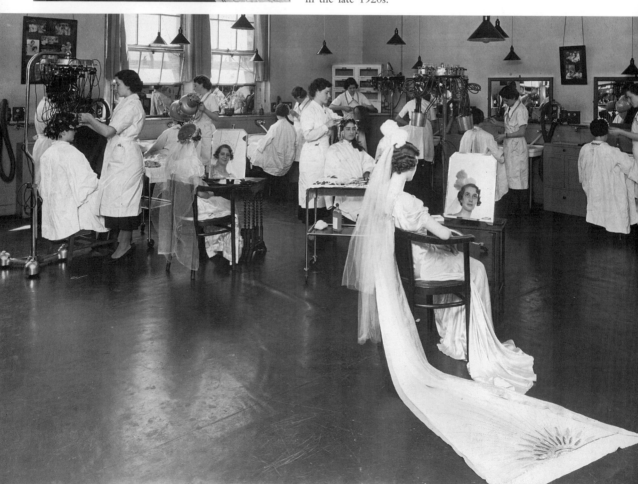

98 & 99 *Left and below left.* In common with all London needle-trade schools, both Shoreditch and Clapham Trade Schools had annual exhibitions of work which were shown to parents, guardians, prospective employers, LCC officials, the consultative committees and all those with an interest in the schools. Fig. 98 shows the dressmaking students at Shoreditch with one of their garments while Fig. 99 displays both the dressmaking and millinery work done at Clapham. Both photographs were taken *c.*1930.

100 *Below.* The dressmaking class at Clapham Trade School in October 1930. The garment on the stand in the centre of the photograph is bias cut. Cutting material on the cross rather than on the lengthwise grain was pioneered by Madeleine Vionnet in Paris and widely copied. It meant that clothes were moulded to the body contours, so displaying the outlines of the wearer's natural figure. These garments were not worn with heavy corsets. Examples of this new approach to dressmaking, which was very difficult to execute, can be seen in many of the photographs of the students' work.

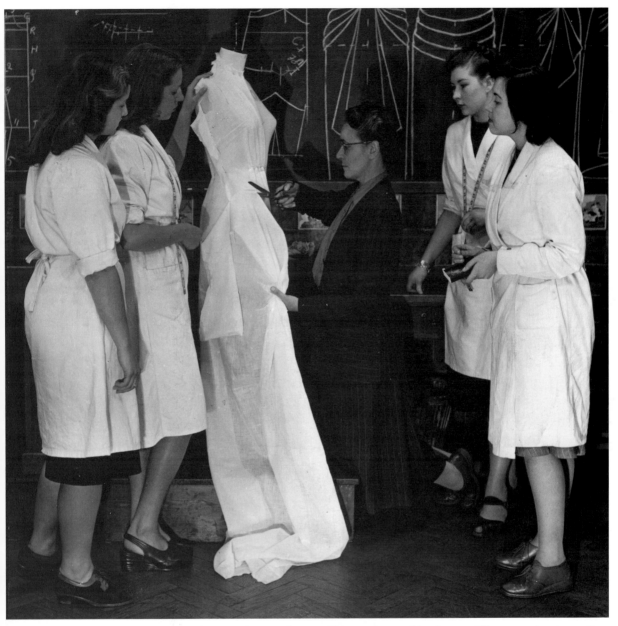

101 *Above left*. Students' work in the early 1930s showing the use of bias cutting, resulting in very different evening dresses from the previous decade.

102 *Far left*. Three evening gowns designed and made by Barrett Street students in the early 1930s. The bias cutting and draped styles of the 1930s lent themselves to being modelled 'on-the-stand'. Modelling on-the-stand involved interpreting a fashion sketch into a three-dimensional design which was achieved by pinning, draping and cutting a soft cotton fabric, usually Leno or Mull, on a tailor's-stand until the desired effect was obtained. The fabric was then marked ready to be used as a pattern. This was a technique in which many of the dressmaking trade teachers excelled.

103 *Left*. Rita Clover, a student at Barrett Street, modelling on-the-stand in the early 1950s. Although former dressmaking senior and evening class students testify to learning modelling on-the-stand in the 1930s, the archive has no photographs of it being carried out in the inter-war period.

104 *Above*. Miss Peake, dressmaking teacher at Barrett Street, demonstrating modelling on-the-stand in *c*.1950.

105 *Top, far left*. Three evening gowns. The two photographed from the back view have a décolletage back.

106 *Top, left*. Two student mannequins modelling evening dresses, *c*.1930s. The dress on the left is partly made in a floral print with two ruffles near the hem line. Floral prints were becoming increasingly popular in this decade.

107 *Bottom left*. Student and child mannequins. The high-waisted puffed-sleeved dress of the child is typical of the period. According to former students many children's clothes were made, commissioned by friends of the staff, members of the LCC and the Trades Consultative Committee.

108 *Bottom, right*. Two 1930s cotton evening dresses, one with cap sleeves and waist sash tied in a bow, the other in a large floral print with ruffled trimmed peplum and neckline. The dress on the right shows clearly the very narrow hand-worked hem on the sleeves, sash and hem.

109 *Below*. Six students modelling examples of work done at Barrett Street, *c*.1930s. We have no information on the gentleman in the photograph; possibly he was a member of the school's Needle-trades Consultative Committee.

110 Fur trimmed evening coat and full–length low cut evening dress, *c*.1934, worn with a necklace.

111 & 112 Two views showing an evening gown with train early in the 1930s. This style lends itself to being modelled on the stand.

113 & 114 Two bias cut evening gowns, *c*.1934. The diagonal seaming on the hips in Fig. 114 emphasises the fullness in the lower skirt. The matching shoulder cape is trimmed with fur.

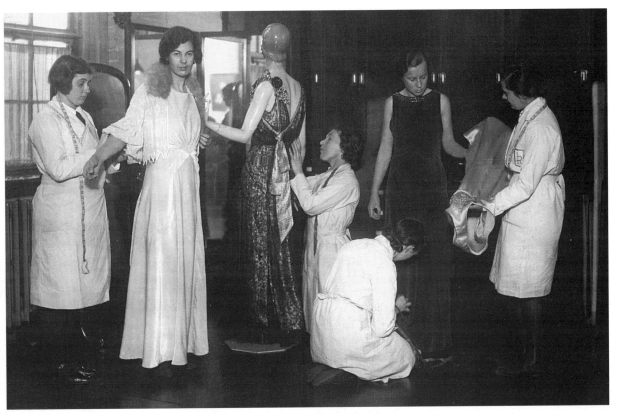

115 Students working in the 1930s.

116 The dressmaking room with an example of day and evening wear, *c.*1934.

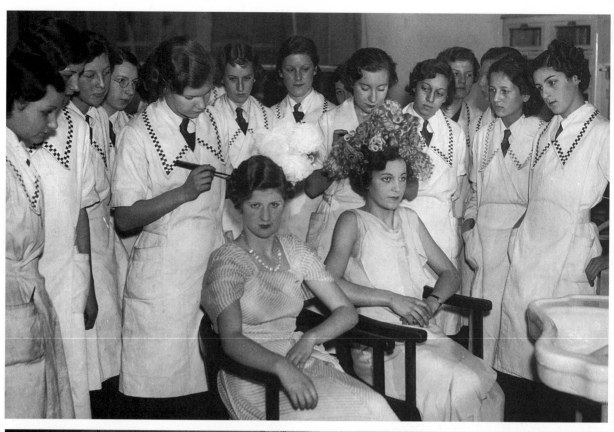

117 *Left*. Hairdressing students preparing mannequins for the annual exhibition of 1934. The mannequin on the left in the capped sleeve dress is having her hair dressed using marcel irons.

118 *Below left*. Mannequins displaying dresses designed and made by senior dressmaking students, *c*.1934.

119 & 120 *Right and below*. West End department stores and the fashionable dress houses made much bridal wear which therefore was produced by the students of Barrett Street. This photograph shows bridal wear designed and made by Barrett Street students in the mid-1930s.

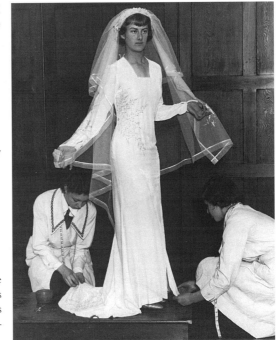

121 The hand embroidery and tambour class of 1936. As well as a consultative committee responsible for overseeing the trade curriculum in all LCC needle-trades school, each needle-trade school had its committee responsible for ensuring that the schools were training girls in the areas that the trade required. This close link with the fashion industry made trade schools very commercially aware in this era, training to the exact requirements of the trade.

122 The senior art class at Barrett Street in the mid–1930s. The evening gown being drawn on the left appears in Fig. 143.

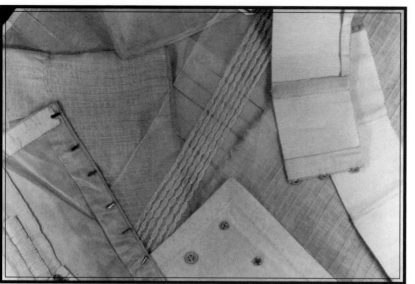

123-28 Miss Mary Wildman, a junior dressmaking student at Barrett Street between 1936 and 1938, donated to the college archive the samples of stitches and sewing techniques she produced in the first term at Barrett Street. After her two-year training Mary went to work for a dressmaker in Margaret Street and then went into the workroom at Debenhams and Freebody. Both jobs were found for her by Mrs. Wells, her trade dressmaking teacher. She was paid 18s. a week.

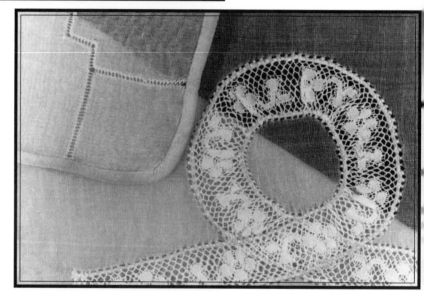

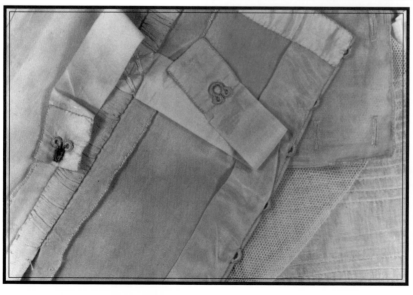

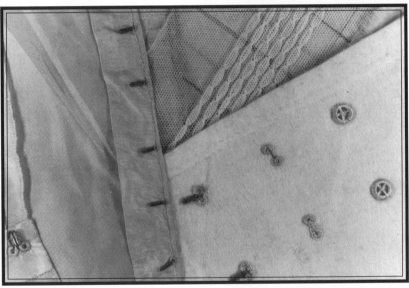

129 The senior dress-making class preparing for the dress parade in 1936. The suit, worn by the mannequin at the back of the classroom, appears in Fig. 131.

130 In May 1936 Barrett Street celebrated its 21st birthday. In December that year the senior school presented its first dress parade, with a commentary in French and English. Garments had traditionally been modelled by mannequins for viewing at the annual exhibition of work, but this was the first time a dress parade was staged. The girl in the ballet dress was Tess, the daughter of the senior LCC Art Inspector at the time.

131 Another photograph of the 1936 dress parade. *The Times* reported the previous year that much of the material used in the senior school was provided by leading British manufacturers and West End stores. It added that West End firms had a tradition of attending the annual exhibition of work to select their future employees.

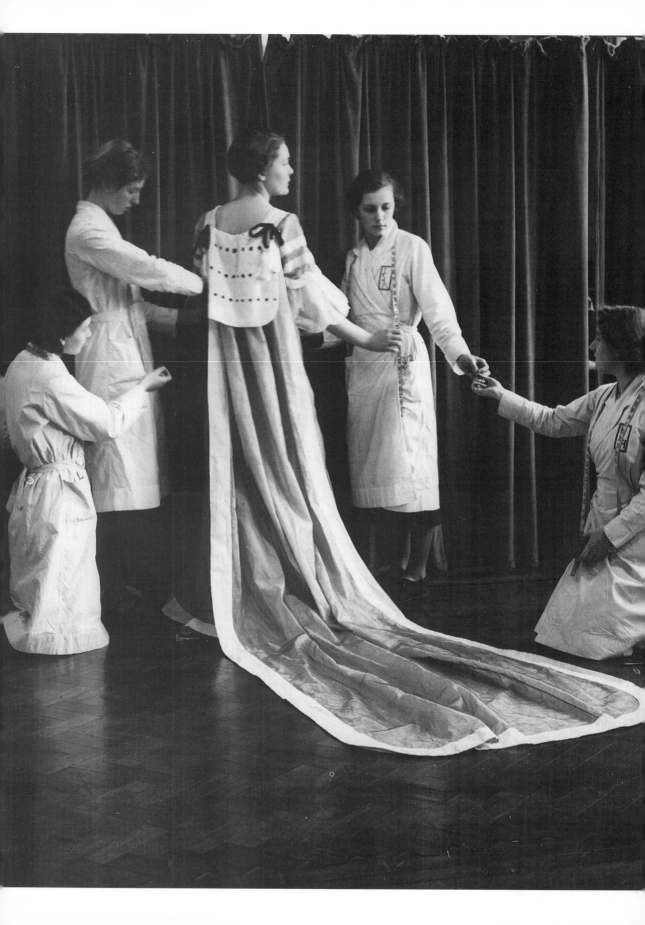

132–34 Students making and sketching peeresses' coronation trains and shoulder capes in 1937, the year that George VI was crowned. The trains were made of crimson velvet lined with white silk. Traditionally the cape was made of miniver with rows of ermine, but it was more likely that the students used rabbit painted with black spots. George VI's coronation was the last at which women who attended Westminster Abbey, and did not have official robes, wore full court dress.

135 As well as forming an integral part of the day courses, evening courses in the history of Dress were held at Barrett Street. One series, 'The Influence of Historic Costume on Modern Dress', advertised the lectures as being illustrated by slides and practical demonstrations in modelling and draping. This photograph shows evening-class students at Barrett Street sketching a replica of Elizabethan costume.

136 & 137 Mock up of the programmes for the 1937 Annual Exhibition and Dress Parade which was not used.

138 The following eight photographs show garments designed and made by senior students of Barrett Street for the 1937 dress parade. The programme for the dress parade, which has been preserved in the archive, shows the wide range of firms that donated fabric for the students' use. This photograph shows two town dresses and two suits, one worn with a pixie hat, made in material donated by Messrs. Galloway.

139 Student mannequin modelling a sunbathing suit. A former student on the junior course remembers this suit being made and described it as 'rather bold'. The work of junior trade students was not normally shown in the dress parades but continued to be shown in the annual exhibitions.

140 *Above*. Evening wear made in materials donated by Vivian Porter, the West End couture house.

141 *Right*. A bridal gown and bridesmaid dresses.

142 *Above left.* A court gown shown in the 1937 dress parade. Although this court dress still has the obligatory train, veil and feathers, the style of the dress is very much of the period.

143 *Above right.* An evening gown with head dress and short tuile veil.

144 *Top right.* A peasant dance put on for the 1937 annual exhibition and dress parade, showing the costumes made by the students. Toward the end of the 1930s until the Second World War broke out this annual event was very elaborate.

145 *Right.* Four 18th-century costumes made and worn by students dancing a minuet to recorders for the 1937 annual exhibition.

146 In March 1936 Barrett Street staged a mime and model entertainment for the LCC jubilee celebration. This entertainment was intended to show the work that was carried out by students in their trade classes. It was so successful that it was copied for the annual exhibition. The last recorded staging of such an entertainment was in Warship Week during the Second World War when the school was evacuated to Maidenhead.

147 Students' doing tambour embroidery. This type of embroidery done with the fabric stretched across a frame. Tambour embroidery uses a special needle; the stitch resembles a conventional chain-stitch.

148 The embroidery class, *c.*1938.

149   *Above.* The dressmaking class at Barrett Street, *c.*1938.

150   *Above right.* The 1938 programme for the annual exhibition and dress parade states that all the student models have taken a course in deportment and modelling. The following ten photographs show the clothes designed and made by senior school students and modelled in the dress parade.

151   *Right.* Coats made by the tailoring students in 1938. As stated in the programme, the material for these outfits was donated by the National Association of Scottish Woollen Manufacturers.

EXHIBITION

The Students will be engaged at their respective trades.

MAIN BUILDING.

Top Floor—

Room 16 } Dressmaking Junior Tech. 2nd year.
15 }

14 Ladies' Tailoring Junior T. 2nd year.

18 Embroidery (Hand).

17 Studio—(Design) All Trades.

Middle Floor—

Hairdressing—

10 Saloon Junior Tech. 2nd year.

9 „ Senior Tech.

8 Board Work.

11 Trade Science.

12 Manicure and Face Massage.

Dressmaking—

13 Junior Tech. 1st year.

First Floor—

6 Machine Embroidery.

5 General Education and French.

Hall—

Dress Parade.

Ground Floor—

Refectory where tea will be served in the afternoon

MAYFAIR ANNEXE—Opposite the Main Building Senior Tech. Dressmaking Room. Students' Common Room where tea will be served in the afternoon

Tea at 3.45 p.m.

Notes on the Dress Parade

Nos.

1—9 A group of models made from material given by the NATIONAL ASSOCIATION OF SCOTTISH WOOLLEN MANUFACTURERS. These would provide an excellent day-time outfit for all occasions. The materials shewn in this group demonstrate the versatility of woollen fabrics made in Scotland to-day.

10—16 A group of LONDON CLOTHES including walking, day and afternoon dresses and four models made from material given by BROCKLEHURST-WHISTON AMALGAMATED LTD.—an interesting Tussore suit of silk woven in England, two dresses of MACCLESFIELD SILK and a two colour tennis outfit of sharkskin.

17—22 Models made in CREASE RESISTING LINEN given by THE IRISH LINEN GUILD. This group provides suggestions for every occasion on a summer cruise.

28—33 ORGANDIE presented by Messrs. JACOBY-IKLÉ is used for this group. It includes organdie printed in exquisite designs and embroidered in colour, shewing it to be a material suitable for varied occasions and for wearers of many ages.

36—37 The charm of velvet is demonstrated in models made from material presented by Messrs. PELTZER-LISTER VELVET CO., LTD.

38—40 A gay group of evening dresses made from material given by BRITISH CELANESE LTD. These models are an excellent illustration of the clear and vivid colours to be found in RAYON fabrics.

42—44 Three dresses made from RAYON FABRICS given by Messrs. COURTAULDS, LTD. This group contains a simple dance frock and a Court dress suggesting the wide range of purposes for which these materials can be used.

L.C.C.
Barrett
Street
Technical
School
Oxford
Street
West 1.

INVITATION

to

Annual Exhibition
and
Dress Parade

on

WEDNESDAY, Dec. 14th, 1938

2 - 4.30 p.m.

PLEASE PRESENT THIS PROGRAMME FOR ADMISSION

The Exhibition will be open also on Wednesday, Dec. 14th, and Thursday, Dec. 15th, 6 - 8.30 p.m. when no ticket will be required for admission.

152 & 153 *Above left and right.* Suits and afternoon dresses. The two striped dresses are made of Macclesfield silk.

154 *Left.* Children's clothes, 1937. Single buttoned wool coat with two dresses in cotton organdie with fine ruffles and pin tucks.

155 *Right.* These outfits are described in the programme as cruise wear. The long dress is made from linen donated by the Irish Linen Guild.

157 Silk velvet and taffeta evening gown with one shoulder strap, the velvet dinner gown with draped sleeves.

158 An ice-blue satin court gown. The diamante embroidery was carried out by junior school pupils.

159 & 160 As is the tradition, Barrett Street finished its 1938 dress parade with a satin bridal gown. The programme states that the dress was in silver grey and features a nun's hood.

161-63 These photographs were taken and distributed by the Ministry of Information during the Second World War. Before the Second World War, many Barrett Street pupils were Jewish—large numbers of Jewish men and women worked in the West End needle trades. According to former pupils, Miss Cox had close links with various Jewish philanthropic organisations. Former Jewish refugees who attended the school testify to her warm welcome. One former student, who fled Germany with her family just before the onset of the war and subsequently settled in Israel, regularly kept in contact with Miss Cox until her death in the late 1960s. These three photographs show Amelia Gans, a Dutch Jewish girl, who settled in London with her family. Her brother Maurice was in the Royal Dutch Army stationed in Britain.

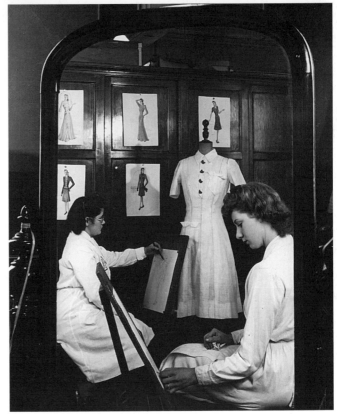

164   This photograph shows a ready-to-wear class in 1947. During 1942/3 The Board of Trade commissioned the British Standards Institute to produce a set of standard measurements for the ready-to-wear trade. The resultant standardisation sizing chart can be seen on the wall. During the 1950s Shoreditch Girls' Trade School was renamed Shoreditch College for the Garment Trades and continued to expand courses in ready-to-wear clothing, training both men and women.

165 & 166 The work of Barrett Street students in the 1950s. Barrett Street, which was renamed Barrett Street Technical College, continued to train women and, after the retirement of Miss Cox, men also began to work in the couture trade. In 1967 the college merged with Shoreditch College for the Garment Trades when it was felt that the clothing industry would be better served by one college for the fashion trade. The Inner London Education Authority [ILEA] press release of July 1966 reads as follows:

> The reason for the proposal is that considerable changes have been taking place in the two industries over the past few years. The development of new techniques and methods of production are breaking down the divisions which have formally existed between fashion as represented by the couture and bespoke houses and the manufacture of clothing generally.

So ended an era of unique collaboration between the LCC needle-trade schools and the luxury couture trade.

INDEX

Roman numerals refer to pages in the introduction and arabic numerals to individual illustrations.